BEAUTIFUL
BRAIDS

Hair Designer
MARY BETH JANSSEN-FLEISCHMAN

Contributing Writer
JUDY RAMBERT

PUBLICATIONS INTERNATIONAL, LTD.

Hair Designer MARY BETH JANSSEN-FLEISCHMAN is International Artistic Director for Pivot Point International Inc. and Artistic Director for Design Forum Publication.

Contributing Writer JUDY RAMBERT is Vice-President of Education for Pivot Point International Inc.

Photographer
IRENA LUKASIEWICZ

Models
BARB HORN/Royal Model
    Management
LISA MYLES/Royal Model
    Management
DONNA WIECZORKOWSKI

Pictured on front cover, clockwise from top left: Casual Grace (see page 8), New and Glamorous (see page 19), Streamlined variation (see page 60), and Couture (see page 45).

Pictured on back cover: Pattern Play (see page 54).

CONTENTS

INTRODUCTION 3

OVERVIEW OF TECHNIQUES 4

HINTS AND TIPS 6

CASUAL GRACE
Overbraid 8

CLASSIC BEAUTY
Overbraid Chignon 11

FREEDOM BRAID
Accent Overbraid 13

SOFT AND SHAPELY
Inverted Overbraid 16

NEW AND GLAMOROUS
Inverted Overbraid with Curls 19

TAILORED ELAN
Inverted Overbraid—Tucked Under 23

ELEGANT SIMPLICITY
Underbraid 25

ACTIVE HAIR
Projected Underbraid 28

TEXTURAL INTEREST
Multiple Underbraids 32

SOPHISTICATE
Ribbon Underbraid 37

LAVISH DETAIL
Two-Strand Overlap—Free 41

COUTURE
Two-Strand Overlap—Tucked Under 45

OPULENT
Reverse Overlap with Double Rolls 47

LUXURIOUS
Variation: Reverse Overlap with Single Roll 52

PATTERN PLAY
Two-Strand Hairline Twist 54

STREAMLINED
Two-Strand Rope 58

ELEGANT STATURE
Twisted Roll 61

INTRODUCTION

Designing long hair is an art form that dates back before Egyptian times and continues through history as a barometer of fashion. Classic hair designs are altered to reflect the current mood or fashion statement of the day, but the basic techniques that are used don't vary much. It's the combination of techniques you use, where you use them on your head, or the accessories you choose that create the trend interpretation.

Long hair techniques are fun, and you can create many designs at home once you have devoted some time to practicing. The designs featured in this book have been created by a very skilled professional, so don't be discouraged if your initial results are not an exact duplicate. As in any art form, the more you practice the better you become. The purpose of this book is to show you some classic techniques that you can use on yourself, your friends, or your family between professional salon visits. So have some fun, experiment with the designs we feature and create some of your own.

BRAIDING

Two basic techniques create three-strand braided designs. One is **overbraiding**, and the other is **underbraiding**. In overbraiding, the outside strands are crossed over the center strand. The pattern is reversed in underbraiding; outside strands are crossed under the center strand.

Braids created with an overbraid technique have also been called English braids; those with an underbraid technique have been called Dutch braids. The choice between overbraiding or underbraiding depends upon your personal preference and which technique is more comfortable for you to perform.

Overbraiding

Underbraiding

When these two techniques are performed on free-hanging ponytails, there is only a slight difference in the braided pattern. The visible difference occurs when these techniques are combined with the addition of new sections of hair gathered from the scalp and added to the outside strands while you continue to braid.

Overbraiding with added sections, which is also known as a French braid, produces a flat or **inverted braid** pattern.

When you incorporate new sections of hair while underbraiding, the result will be a raised or **projected braid.** This technique creates corn-row designs, along with many other styles.

OVERVIEW OF TECHNIQUES

TWO-STRAND OVERLAP

This technique features only two strands, which are alternately crossed from one side to the other side. The technique can be performed on the free ends of a pony-tail or along the scalp with new sections added. The result is a beautiful herringbone pattern, which has also been called a fish tail.

TWISTS

Individual strands can be twisted independently, or two strands can be twisted together. The resulting pattern resembles a rope. This technique can be performed on the free ends of a ponytail, or the twist can be combined with new additions picked up along the hairline that are incorporated into the twist.

All of the hair designs included in this book are created with these basic techniques.

HINTS AND TIPS

To help you get started and to make it easier to learn the designs included in this book, try these suggestions and professional "inside tips."

PRODUCTS

Pomade

Use a pomade to remove static, control flyaway ends, and add a glossy sheen to either straight or curly hair. Pomade should be used sparingly, though. Apply a very small amount to one hand and liquefy it between your palms. Then run your hands through the hair before braiding or for small touch-ups afterward.

Gel

Gel will control hair lengths too, but it produces more of a wet effect than pomade does. You can apply gel to all of the hair before you braid, or, when you want a clean, off-the-face effect, you can apply it to the perimeter hairline where lengths tend to be shorter.

Gel can also be used after a braid is finished to smooth down loose or uncontrolled hairs. Apply it to your fingertip or to the end of a hairpin; then smooth it on top of the stray hairs to encourage them back into the braided pattern.

Hair Spray

Besides using hair spray to hold the finished design in place, try using it in spot areas as you work. Also, if you want a soft finish but need to control the hair, spray into the palm of your hand and then smooth over the surface of the hair to control flyaway strands before you braid.

Coated Bands

Ordinary rubber bands can place undue tension on the hair, which may cause hair breakage. Using a coated rubber band to secure ponytails and the ends of a braid will reduce the stress on the hair. This extra consideration will help keep your hair in better condition.

ACCESSORIES

Adding an ornament, barrette, ribbon, or any of the wide assortment of accessories available can finish your completed design. The selection is based on practical purposes—to keep ends secure—as well as decorative options. Both the occasion and your wardrobe should influence the type of accessory you select.

For business, simplicity is generally the key. For active sports, choose barrettes, grips, or ribbons that adhere with tension. For special occasions, pearls or silver and gold ornaments give extra elegance and sophistication. And don't forget a great standby—flowers, either fresh or silk. From large dahlias to smaller baby's breath, flowers pinned into the design can add a romantic look.

Remember, not every design requires accessorizing; sometimes the pattern in the hair is enough. If you do choose ornamentation, make sure that it matches the feeling that you want to portray based on your mood or what you're wearing. Avoid clashing or looking so busy that the total look is lost.

Your professional salon, as well as hobby craft stores, fabric stores, and millinery sections of departments stores, can all be resources for you to find the right accessory to add the final touch to your design for long hair.

COVERING PONYTAIL BASES

Hair Wrapping

An excellent tip for a more dressed look is to cover the band with hair.

Select a small portion of hair from underneath the ponytail.

Wrap the hair around the base of the ponytail to hide the covered band.

Fasten the wrap by inserting a hairpin.

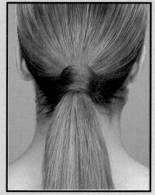

The result is a simple, yet beautiful complement to any design.

Spiral Wrapping

By wrapping a cord or ribbon in a spiral fashion around the braid ends, you can cover a band or even eliminate it entirely.

   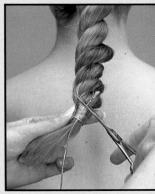

Select a long cord, at least ten or twelve inches in length. Loop one end and hold it next to the ends of the hair.

Wrap the loose end around the hair from the bottom upward. When you get toward the top and enough of the loop is still showing, insert the end of the cord through the loop.

Hold this end as shown, and pull slowly on the bottom free end of the cord until the loop disappears into the inside of the wrapped area.

Clip off the extra cord ends on both sides.

The result looks more difficult than it really is. Vary the effect by using different types of cord or ribbon to complement your wardrobe or reflect the mood of the finished design.

7

CASUAL GRACE
OVERBRAID

Overbraiding is the most commonly used braiding technique, probably because it seems to be the easiest to execute. Once the hair is divided into three strands, the outside strands are crossed over the center strand. This produces a braided pattern that appears flat; it is sometimes referred to as an English braid. Try this technique first with a ponytail until you are comfortable with the path the strands need to travel. Once you are familiar with the technique and experiment with it, you'll find that the options for using overbraiding within a hair design are endless.

1. Before beginning, comb the hair smooth to ensure a neat braid. All the techniques featured in this book are demonstrated on dry hair, but you can also braid the hair while it is damp. The results will be softer on dry hair and tighter on damp hair.

2. Position a ponytail in the crown—the topmost part of the head—and divide it into three strands of equal size. A small amount of gel could be applied to the hair at this point to control stray ends.

3. Cross the right strand over the center strand. The center strand moves to the right and the right strand now becomes the center strand.

4. Reach across to the left and cross the left strand over the center strand. The left strand should now be in the center position.

5. Repeat this basic pattern. Use your thumb and index finger to grasp the outside strands and cross them to the center position.

6. Your braids will be neater if you slide your hand down the length of the strand every so often to blend and untangle stray hairs. Hold two strands tightly in one hand so that the other hand is free to smooth down the length of the remaining strand.

(continued)

7. Try to maintain tension as you braid. It is helpful to keep your fingers close to the braided area and use your little finger to anchor the strands.

8. Continue this basic pattern, remembering that outside strands are alternately crossed over the center strand and trade positions with it. If the ends poke out from the braid as you work, try applying a small amount of gel to encourage them to blend into the pattern.

9. Secure the ends with a covered band. Ribbon can be tied around the ponytail at the beginning and also at the end of the braid to finish the look, if desired.

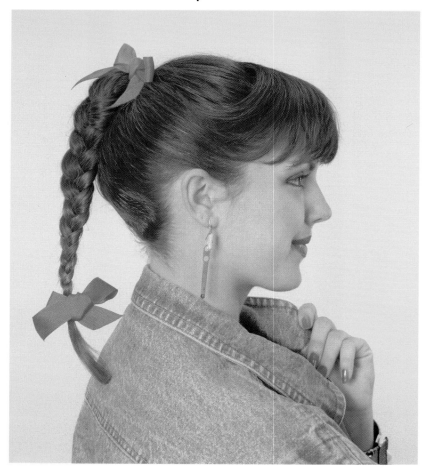

CLASSIC BEAUTY
OVERBRAID CHIGNON

Once you have created an overbraid, you can quickly transform it into a classic chignon. The main requirement for this design is a braided length that is long enough to turn a complete circle around the base of a ponytail and allow the ends to be tucked under. Vary the expression of this design by changing the location of the ponytail from the crown of the head to the nape—the back of the neck. If you have shorter lengths around the face, they can be left out of the ponytail and styled independently.

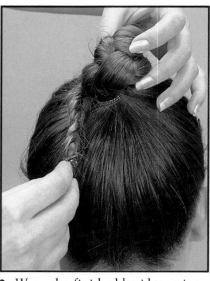

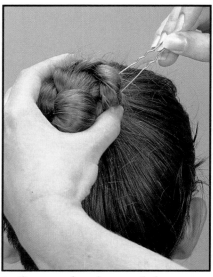

1. Begin this design by positioning a ponytail on the crown and then using the overbraiding technique to braid the remaining lengths. Secure the ends with a small covered band.

2. Wrap the finished braid, curving it around the base of the ponytail. The center will rise upward slightly. That's supposed to happen to achieve the shape of this chignon.

3. Cup one hand around the chignon, and then secure its position by inserting a large hairpin into the coil and the hair underneath it.

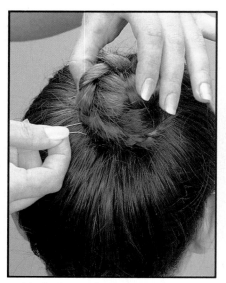

4. Tuck the ends under and secure them with small bobby pins. If the hair is very heavy, you may achieve a better hold with large pins or several small ones.

5. Balance the volume of the design by inserting a hairpin into any low areas and lifting the hair outward. Spray with hair spray to hold the new shape.

6. Shorter bang lengths were left out of the ponytail and styled smooth, but if your hair is longer at the front you can style it off the face and include it in the ponytail. Accessories and ornaments are optional on the finished design.

FREEDOM BRAID
ACCENT OVERBRAID

Besides being attractive, this design is great for activities such as aerobics, since it secures hairline lengths and keeps them from falling in your face. It's also a quick design alternative for younger girls who like simplicity. As this braid is created, strands of hair are picked up from the hairline and joined into one side of the braid. You could vary the design by braiding both hairlines or combining more than one braid on each side. This technique can be used successfully on a variety of hair textures, but it does require that the hair at the sides be jaw-length or longer.

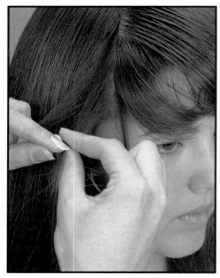

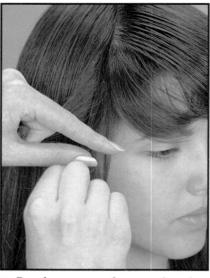

1. Begin by combing the side so that the hair falls naturally. Part off a small triangular section. The size of the section can be altered to correspond to the size of the braid you would like to create. Divide this section into three equal-size strands, and position your fingers close to the hairline.

2. Reach across to the strand at the hairline—here the right strand—and grasp it with your thumb and index finger.

3. Cross the right strand over the center strand. The center strand moves to the right, and the right strand becomes the center strand.

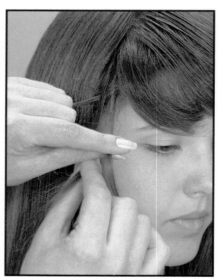

4. Now cross the left strand over the center. The left strand now becomes the center strand.

5. Repeat the pattern by crossing the right strand over the center once again. Then pull the strands taut.

6. Now that one overbraid sequence is complete, pick up a section of hair from along the hairline and add it to the left strand.

7. Use your thumb and index finger to grasp this new combined strand, and cross it over to the center position. Avoid lifting the hair away from the hairline.

8. Cross the right strand over the center. Hair will not be added to the right strand during this technique.

9. Try to keep the width of the picked-up sections on the left side consistent. You may find it helpful to define the size of the braid by parting through the entire area and then tucking the remaining lengths behind the ear to keep them out of your way.

10. Always cross the new section over the center. Maintain tension on the strands to keep the braid secure.

11. Once you reach the end of the hairline, continue with the basic overbraid technique. Use your thumb and index fingers to grasp outside strands and cross them over the center.

12. Braid to the ends. Although very tiny braids on curly hair may not unravel, you will usually need to secure the ends. Use the spiral wrapping technique shown here (see pages 6 and 7) or a small covered band.

SOFT AND SHAPELY
INVERTED OVERBRAID

This design is most often called a French braid. It's created using a variation of the basic overbraiding technique in which new sections of hair are gathered and added to the outside strands as you braid. Outside strands get larger as you braid and are always crossed over the center strand. This results in an inverted braided pattern that lies flat on the head. A centered braid is the most common, but it's only one of the many designs you can create with this technique.

1. Begin by sectioning a triangle at the front hairline. Divide the section into three equal-size strands.

2. Cross the right stand over the center strand. These two strands have now traded places.

3. Now cross the left strand over the center. Use your thumb and index finger to grasp the outside strands and cross them over.

4. Now you will begin gathering new sections of hair and adding them to the outside strands. Begin by dropping the right strand into the hair below.

5. Pick up a new section of hair at the right side from the hairline to the center top of the head. Pick up the right strand you dropped previously along with this new section.

6. Cross this combined strand over the center strand and pull the lengths taut.

(continued)

7. Drop the left strand, pick up a new section, and grasp the combined strand with your thumb and index finger. Cross this combined strand over the center.

8. To keep the braid flat, you must maintain consistent tension and work close to the head. You may find that resting your little fingers on the head helps you to control the tension.

9. Braid close to the head until you reach the crown. Then, instead of following the curve of the head, position your hands along an imaginary line and direct the new sections upward. Lifting the strands away from the head will achieve a draped effect in the hair.

10. As you braid the back, you no longer need to drop the strand that will be combined with the new picked-up section. Hold all three strands in your free hand and use your thumb and index finger to pick up a new section. Direct it upward to join the strand that will be crossed over the center.

11. Once you have picked up all of the hairline lengths, finish the design with the basic overbraiding technique. Cross left over center and then right over center until lengths run out.

12. Secure the ends with a covered band and finish decoratively, if you wish.

NEW AND GLAMOROUS
INVERTED OVERBRAID WITH CURLS

This partially braided design offers a more dressed alternative for those who like to wear their long hair down. The proportion of braided hair to hair that is left down can be varied, but plan the effect in advance so that you can isolate the hair that will not be braided. The basic technique, overbraiding with new hair added to the outside strands, creates an inverted braid pattern that lies flat against the head. Wide picked-up sections result in a bold braid; narrow picked-up sections create a more delicate-looking braid.

1. This design begins with a side part and a sectioning pattern to divide the hair that will be braided from the hair that will fall freely. Clip the lower lengths to keep them out of your way. If you have bangs that will be left out of the braid, you should isolate them also.

2. Begin braiding at the side part by selecting a narrow, triangular section behind the bangs. Divide the section into three equal-size strands. Cross the strand closest to the hairline—here the left strand—over the center strand.

3. Now cross the right strand over the center strand.

4. Release the left strand and allow it to fall into the hair below.

5. Pick up a new section of hair from the hairline to the area where you would like the braid positioned. Gather this section along with the strand just released and smooth down the lengths.

6. Reach over with the opposite thumb and index finger to grasp this new addition.

7. Cross this addition over to the center position.

8. Now drop the right strand. Pick up a new section along with the strand just released.

9. Cross this new addition over the center. Then repeat the pick-up on the left side.

10. Try to keep the size of the picked-up additions as even as possible. Some people like to use their thumbnails to part and control the size of the sections.

11. Use your thumb periodically to separate the sections, and slide your hand down the lengths to control stray hairs.

12. Direct the strands to conform to the curve of the head, and keep your hands close to the head as you braid.

(continued)

13. Continue braiding to the center back.

14. Overbraid the free ends a few times to secure the braid, and clip the ends to secure them temporarily.

15. Repeat the overbraid and pick-up procedure on the opposite side, but on the side away from the part, begin with a narrow rectangular section and braid toward the center back once again.

16. Join the completed braids in the center. Secure them with a covered band to create a ponytail.

17. You can leave the hanging lengths natural, or you can add additional curl with a hot-roller set. If you choose to set your hair, clip the ponytail upward and set the bottom first, using vertical partings.

18. Then set the ponytail portion in the same manner. Choose the size of the hot rollers according to the amount of curl desired. Remove the hot rollers after five to ten minutes, and lightly comb through the curls. Finish the design by covering the ponytail band.

TAILORED ELAN
INVERTED OVERBRAID—TUCKED UNDER

The key element of this overbraiding variation is keeping your hands positioned away from the head so that the finished braid extends from the scalp and creates a draped effect that has volume. The braided ends are tucked under and pinned, which creates a wider shape in the back area of the head. The tucked-in section plumps out the braid pattern. This overbraid variation requires somewhat longer hair to extend out from the head and still be included in the braid. You can begin this technique from the front hairline area or at the top of the head behind a shorter fringe or bangs.

1. Divide a large triangular section into three equal-size sections. The two hands anchor the outside strands, while the thumb and index finger of the left hand hold the center strand. This frees the thumb and index finger of the right hand to begin the overbraiding.

2. Reach over the middle strand to the outside left strand and cross it over to the middle position.

3. Alternate to the opposite side. Reach over with the thumb and index finger, grasp the outside right strand, and bring it over to the middle position.

4. Repeat the pattern, but now pick up new sections (as described on pages 17 and 18) and then join them to the outside strands. Direct the combined strand up and over the center strand to the middle position. Braid to the ends and secure.

5. Begin to roll the ends onto themselves, up and into the inside of the braid.

6. Pin through the underneath side of the braid with a large bobby pin, so that it goes through the roll. Release the roll and tuck it under, letting the overbraid drape around the roll. Secure with extra hairpins, if necessary. A spritz of hair spray gives an extra measure of holding power.

ELEGANT SIMPLICITY
UNDERBRAID

In the underbraiding technique, outside stands are crossed *under* the center strand. This produces a plump-looking braid that is also called a Dutch braid. Begin with a simple ponytail to learn the basics. When you are familiar with the pattern, experiment with it to create your own interpretations. Once mastered, this basic technique can be used alone or in combination with other techniques.

1. Begin by creating a ponytail where you would like the braid positioned. For this design we chose the lower nape. Divide the ponytail into three equal-size strands.

2. Direct the left strand under the center strand. The center strand moves to the left and the left strand becomes the center strand.

3. Reach under the center and grasp the right strand with your thumb and index finger.

4. Direct it under the center. The right strand now exchanges positions with the center strand.

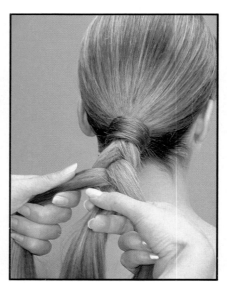

5. Repeat this basic pattern. Direct the left strand under the center strand.

6. Grasp the right strand with your thumb and index finger and direct it under the center.

7. As you braid you will be holding two strands in one hand and one strand in the other hand, which will alternate. Your braids will be neater if you slide your hand down the length of the strands every so often to smooth stray hairs.

8. Smooth the side with one strand as you maintain tension on the other two strands with the other hand.

9. Continue underbraiding down the length of the strands. Finish the braid by securing the ends with a covered band or wrapping them with a cord or thread. This creates the basic style shown on page 25.

10. If your hair is long enough, you can create a chignon. Coil the braid around the base of the ponytail. Hold the braid against the head to keep it flat. Wrap the ends under the braid and tuck them into the center to hide them.

11. Hold the coil with one hand and insert a large hairpin into the chignon to hold it in position. Additional pins will be necessary to secure the chignon if your hair is heavy.

12. This design has a classic appeal and can be varied by changing the location of the chignon and by adding different ornamentation.

This design uses the basic underbraid technique with new sections of hair added in to the outside strands as you braid. The outside strands are always crossed under the center, which results in a braided pattern that projects upward. Adjust the size of the picked-up sections according to the intricacy of the pattern you would like to create. This version positions a single braid down the center from the front hairline to the nape. The same braid can be created from a side part or combined with several small braids positioned across the head. Look at the sample variations on the following pages.

1. Begin at the front hairline and create a triangular section. Divide the section into three equal-size strands. "Right" and "left" in these directions refer to the reader's point of view, since reversing them will not affect the braid.

2. Cross the right strand under the center strand. The right strand now becomes the center strand, and the center strand becomes the right strand.

3. Now cross the left strand under the center strand. This positions the left strand in the center.

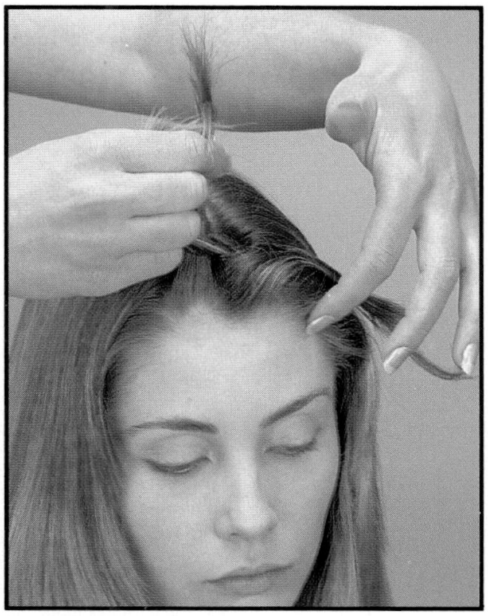

4. Release the right strand.

5. Pick up a new section of hair on the right side from the hairline to the center part. Include the right strand you have just dropped, creating a new combined strand.

6. Shift the center strand to your right hand.

(continued)

7. Extend your thumb and index finger to reach under to grasp the new combined strand.

8. Direct the combined strand under the center and pull the strands taut.

9. Release the left strand and pick up a new section of hair from the hairline to the top of the head.

10. Reach under with your thumb and index finger to grasp the combined strand and cross it under the center.

11. Try to keep the size of the picked-up sections consistent. If you are braiding in shorter layers, you may have to hold the outside strands and direct the new sections upward toward them, rather than releasing the outside strand and picking it back up as you gather the new sections.

12. Pick up the new sections from the hairline to the top of the head and cross them under the center strand.

13. Slide your hand down the strands every so often to untangle and smooth the lengths.

14. Pick up new sections of hair from alternate sides.

15. Clear away the rest of the hair as you hold the new addition with your thumb.

16. Stay close to the head and maintain tension.

17. Once you have picked up the last sections of hair, continue with the basic underbraid pattern on the ends.

18. Secure the ends with a band and cover it decoratively, if you wish.

TEXTURAL INTEREST
MULTIPLE UNDERBRAIDS

Once you've mastered the underbraiding technique, you can use your imag-
ination in creating many different styles. Several rows of underbraids that curve
to the shape of the head create the intricate design seen here. The most won-
derful part of this design is the possibility of dressing it up or down, depending
on whether ornamental accessories are used.

1. Begin by sectioning the hair to correspond to the number of braids you have planned. Here, curved partings pivot from the ear area to create five sections across the head. To control long hair before clipping it out of the way, twist the hair until the tension makes the strand fold.

2. Then circle the hair around the base area to form a coil.

3. Pin in place with a hairpin or bobby pin, depending on the density of hair. Here, large bobby pins are used to control the thick density.

4. The pre-sectioned areas of the design are controlled and ready for braiding. (You can use this quick and easy twisting technique to create its own design.)

5. The basic underbraiding technique will be used, and new sections of hair will be gathered and added to the outside strands. Part out a small section at the hairline, and divide it into three separate strands.

6. Reach underneath to the strand closest to the hairline area. Using the thumb and index finger, cross the strand underneath the center strand. The center strand moves to the right and the right strand becomes the center strand.

(continued)

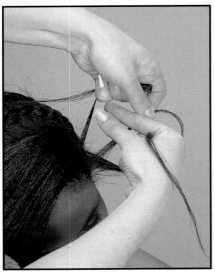

7. Reach under the center strand to the outside left strand.

8. Cross this strand under the center strand so that it becomes the new center strand. Note the use of the thumb and index finger as the key fingers in positioning, holding, and crossing under.

9. Once an initial cross-under is done on both sides, begin picking up new sections of hair within the section that has been parted. With your thumb and index finger, grasp a new section of hair from the center out to the hairline. Join it with the outside strand of the braid to make one strand.

10. Cross this combined strand under the center strand.

11. Repeat this procedure on the opposite side of the braid, picking up a new section and adding it to the outside strand.

12. This combined outside strand is brought under to the center. Position your hands so that you can work with equal tension to make a clean braid. Position your palm toward the head and keep your hand close. Use your thumb and index finger to grasp and pull the outside strands underneath the center strand.

13. Exchange your hand positions to prepare for grasping strands. Your hand anchors the hair, which frees the thumb and index finger and allows them to pick up new sections on the opposite side.

14. Alternate to the opposite side. Pick up, join the picked-up hair to the side strand, and cross under.

15. Continue this technique up and over the head. It is important to keep the partings clean and your hands and fingers close to the head for control, particularly if you are braiding lengths of hair six inches or shorter.

16. Complete the underbraiding, alternating the new picked-up sections from side to side.

17. When all the scalp hair has been picked up, continue the basic underbraiding technique on the remaining lengths. Secure the ends. (For a different look, after all new sections are picked up, you can secure them near the base area and let all the ends fall free.)

18. The five braided ends are crisscrossed over each other.

(continued)

19. Remove the bands securing the ends, and twirl the braided ends around each other as shown to form a braided chignon at the side.

20. Secure this chignon with hairpins and/or bobby pins. In this case, large hairpins work well.

21. The balance of this design with the intricate projected braids can be accessorized with ribbons and ornaments, as well as with a sleek or curly bang.

SOPHISTICATE
RIBBON UNDERBRAID

This design has several themes. The ribbon added into the underbraid adds a spark of color to coordinate with your wardrobe selection. The asymmetry of the underbraid travels from above the eye on one side up over the curve of the head to the opposite side behind the ear. This unique balance adds interest. The longer nape lengths are left loose to be gathered by the braid. Whether straight, wavy, or curly, these ends are fanned out to add volume and fullness. If hair lengths are shorter—four to six inches—this design can also work beautifully with a hairpiece or switch added at the nape area.

1. Begin by sectioning the hair to separate the area to be underbraided from the loose areas. This sectioning can vary depending upon the amount of hair you want to leave loose at the nape.

2. Select a triangular section slightly off center.

3. Divide this section into three strands and tie a ribbon to the center strand, draping it back. Trim the ends of the ribbon as needed. Various sizes and types of ribbon can be chosen to customize the design.

4. The ribbon will follow the path of the center strand. Cross the right strand under the center strand. "Right" and "left" in these directions refer to the reader's point of view.

5. With your thumb and index finger, reach over and grasp the left strand.

6. Direct it under the center strand to the middle position.

7. After one underbraid sequence is complete, new sections will be picked up and added to the outside strands. The thumb combs through the scalp area to the center, picking up the new section. Combine the new section with the outside strand and hook it over your thumb.

8. Your thumb and index finger are now free to grasp the center strand, allowing the opposite thumb and index finger to reach under and grasp the outside strand.

9. Continue this exchange, alternating from side to side.

10. Reach under with the opposite hand and grasp the left outside strand with your thumb and index finger, and cross the strand under to the center position.

11. Continue braiding toward the back of the head. Maintain tension and work close to the head.

12. As you cross the outside strands under the center, try not to let the ribbon roll inside the braid. For the best effect, keep the ribbon visible and lying on top of the strand.

(continued)

13. Continue to pick up new hair sections and add them to the outside strands before crossing under, until you reach the back area where the hair has been divided.

14. At this point, use the basic underbraiding technique through to the ends.

15. Encircle the ends with the ribbon, and tie it into a knot or pin it with a bobby pin.

16. Wrap this braid completely around the loose hair at the nape.

17. Pin in place securely with a hairpin and/or a bobby pin.

18. The ends may be left loose and straight or curled with a curling iron or hot rollers. The ribbon braid could easily be incorporated all the way to the ends, if you wish. You can create more intricacy by adding more braids to the design

LAVISH DETAIL
TWO-STRAND OVERLAP—FREE

The two-strand overlap produces a herringbone pattern in the hair. It looks like an intricate design, but it's actually easier than braiding with three strands. This variation moves from the front hairline down the center toward the back. Shorter lengths around the face can be left free, and you could begin the overlap behind them. Working close to the head and keeping tension on the hair will produce a flat pattern. If you work away from the head, the lengths will drape and fall softly around the hairline. The length of the hair will limit how far you can work from the head and still achieve a successful result.

1. Brush through the hair to eliminate all tangles. Section a triangular shape at the front hairline. Divide it into two equal-size strands.

2. Cross these two strands. It doesn't matter if you cross right over left or left over right. Here we crossed left over right (from the reader's point of view).

3. Pick up a new section of hair from the right side. Use your thumb to part through from the hairline to the top of the head.

4. Reach across with the thumb and index finger of the left hand to grasp the new section.

5. Cross the new section over to the left side and join it with the left strand.

6. Pick up a new section of hair on the left side from the hairline to the top of the head. Cross it over and join it with the right strand.

7. Alternate this basic pick-up-and-cross-over pattern. Try to keep the size of the picked-up sections consistent.

8. Hold the two strands in one hand while you use the thumb or index finger of the opposite hand to part through the hair to select the picked-up sections.

9. Lift the new section upward to the thumb of the hand holding the strands, and then clear away any loose or tangled hair lengths.

10. Grasp the new section and cross it over to the left side. Join it to the left strand.

11. Keep your hands close to the head until you reach the crown area. Then allow your hands to move away from the head. This will achieve a draped effect and add fullness to the design.

12. Direct the picked-up sections upward to your hands. Work along an imaginary plane straight back from the head to keep the pattern consistent.

(continued)

13. After you have picked up all the hair along the hairline, continue the overlap technique on the two strands remaining in your hand. With the two strands in one hand, subdivide a small portion of hair from the left strand.

14. Cross this subdivision over to the right side. Then subdivide a portion of hair from the right side and cross it over to the left. Try to keep these subdivisions equal in size to achieve a consistent pattern.

15. Use your fingers to keep the two strands separate as you cross the subdivisions from one side to the other side.

16. Continue overlapping down the length of the hair. Secure the ends with a covered band.

COUTURE
TWO-STRAND OVERLAP—TUCKED UNDER

Once a two-strand overlap is completed, you can create a more sophisticated version simply by tucking the tail under and pinning it to itself. For this design you must keep your hands away from the head after you reach the crown so that you achieve enough drape in the hair to enclose the "tail."

1. Perform a two-strand overlap from the front hairline to the center nape. Notice how far your hands must stay away from the head to achieve a draped effect.

2. Secure the ends with a covered band.

3. Roll the "tail" under and tuck it inside.

4. Pin the roll to itself with bobby pins to secure it in position.

5. The draped lengths will surround the roll.

6. If you wish, you can completely enclose the roll by pinning the edges of the draped lengths together with a hairpin or two.

OPULENT
REVERSE OVERLAP WITH DOUBLE ROLLS

 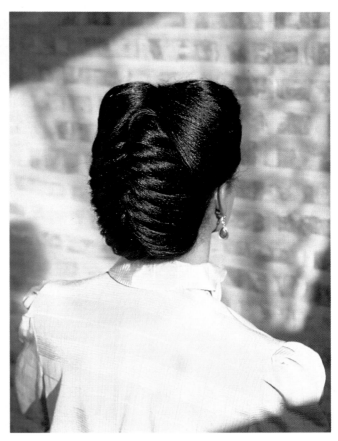

This design uses the overlap technique in a reversed position, working from the nape up toward the crown. It creates a graphic herringbone pattern. You can either work close to the head or, as in this design, slightly away to create an effect with more volume. The number of picked-up sections that you gather will determine the intricacy of the pattern. The rolls in the top front area on either side balance the design in an asymmetrical fashion. You can also use a single roll, as in the style variation on page 52, or if the lengths are shorter, they can be waved or curled.

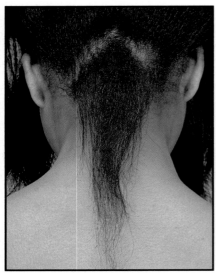

1. Begin at the nape area by releasing a triangular section of hair.

2. Divide this triangular section into two equal-size strands.

3. Cross one side over the other for the first overlap. Here, the right strand was crossed over the left (from the reader's point of view).

4. Now pick up a new section of hair from the left, sectioning from the hairline to the center back as shown.

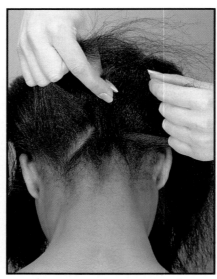

5. Free the thumb and index finger of your right hand so that you can reach over and grasp the new section.

6. Cross this new section over to the right side and join it to the right strand.

7. Pick up a new section on the right side, sectioning from the hairline to the center back.

8. Reach over and grasp this new section, cross it over and join it with the left strand.

9. Remember that you are always working with two strands in your hands and that the picked-up hair is crossed over and joined with the strand on the opposite side. This creates the overlap pattern.

10. As you work up the back of the head, continue to pick up new sections that extend from the hairline to the center back of the head.

11. Reach over for these picked-up sections and overlap them to the opposite side.

12. The herringbone pattern begins to develop.

(continued)

13. If you want extra volume, you can start to move away from the head with the overlap, so that when the overlap is finished it drapes and stands out from the head.

14. Here you can see the final pick-up and overlap in the back area.

15. The ends can be finished off in many ways. Here we've chosen to do a two-strand rope to the ends (see pages 59 and 60). Note that the index finger is positioned inside the crossover area of the two-strand rope before twisting. This ensures even tension.

16. Work this two-strand roping technique to the ends and fasten.

17. The fastened end is circled around and tucked into the gap of the overlap area at the crown.

18. Fasten this topknot with a bobby pin to secure it.

19. To create the rolls, the long hair in the front is parted down the side. Rolls can also be created on shorter hair with lengths of four to six inches.

20. Position a comb at the curve of the head and direct the ends up. This controls the top area and ensures smoothness.

21. Roll the ends under until they reach the scalp area.

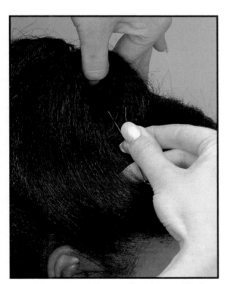

22. Pin securely inside this rolled area with a bobby pin, and insert your fingers to slightly fan the roll outward.

23. Use this same technique on the opposite side.

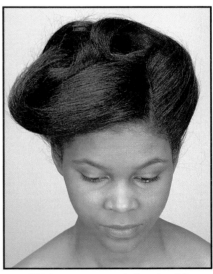

24. We've positioned the double rolls asymmetrically, and they join with the end of the reverse overlap at the crown. You can place the rolls higher or lower, around the hairline, if you wish.

LUXURIOUS
VARIATION: REVERSE OVERLAP WITH SINGLE ROLL

This variation combines the reverse overlap with a single roll. The free ends of the roll create a fringe accent along the forehead. This is a controlled design that is excellent in business situations as well as for going out for the evening. The single roll could also be used throughout the entire back area.

1. Once the back hair has been styled in a reverse overlap, distribute the front hair out from the curve of the head as shown.

2. Lightly twist the hair ends as you hold the hair with one hand near the base. Begin to direct the twist toward the forehead.

3. Roll the hair with some tension toward the front.

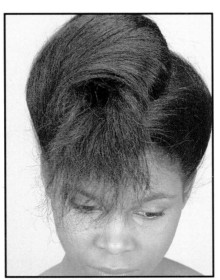

4. Secure inside the roll with a large bobby pin. Add hairpins or bobby pins as needed to secure the roll.

5. The ends are now extending onto the forehead, ready for further styling. They can also be styled straight.

6. Curl the ends as necessary. You can add ornamentation, if you wish.

PATTERN PLAY
TWO-STRAND HAIRLINE TWIST

The two-strand twist is a fairly simple technique that involves separating two strands with your index finger and then turning your hand from a palm-up to a palm-down position. This turn of the wrist produces a twisted pattern in the hair. You must remember to reposition your index finger prior to each turn; otherwise the pattern won't be consistent. For this design, you will always be working with two strands, but they will get larger as you gather hair from along the hairline and add it to one side. Keep your hands close to the head to achieve a tightly twisted pattern.

1. Begin by combing the hair as it would fall naturally. Part a small section of hair at the hairline where the pattern is to begin. Here, we started behind the bangs.

2. If you want to incorporate the bangs into the twist, part a triangular section directly off the part.

3. Direct the beginning section downward, toward the hairline, and divide it into two strands.

4. Insert your index finger between the two strands with your palm facing upward. Don't forget this step; it is very important to the appearance of the twist.

5. Rotate your hand so that the palm is now facing downward. This will automatically position the strands in the twisted pattern.

6. Release the underneath strand and pick up a new section of hair from along the hairline. Combine these together.

(continued)

7. Extend your finger between the new combined strand and the top strand.

8. Turn your hand over so that your palm is facing downward.

9. Repeat the release, pick-up, and twist steps as you follow along the hairline. Use your thumb and index finger to select the new sections from the remaining hair.

10. Remember to extend your index finger between the two main strands with your palm facing upward.

11. Turn your hand over so that your palm is down.

12. Keep your hands close to the hairline and avoid lifting the lengths as you repeat this procedure.

13. Continue picking up hair from the hairline until you reach the center back. Then use the basic two-strand twist technique, without picking up new hair, down the remaining lengths.

14. Once you reach the ends, secure them with a small covered band.

15. Repeat the twisting technique on the opposite side. Follow the hairline once again, and try to match the size of the picked-up sections on this side with the completed side.

16. Remember to position your index finger between the strands with your palm facing upward.

17. Turn your hand over to a palm-down position. Continue around to the center back.

18. When the twist is complete, curve the free ends of the twist into a coil behind the ear. Use a bobby pin to secure it to the head. Coil and pin the twist on the opposite side. Pin the edges of the coils together where they meet.

STREAMLINED
TWO-STRAND ROPE

This classic-looking braid variation is based on two strands instead of three. Each strand is independently twisted, and then the two strands are twisted together. This double twist produces a rounded appearance resembling a rope. A successful pattern depends upon remembering to twist the strand that is on top and to twist in one direction only.

1. Divide the ponytail into two equal-size strands. Slide your hands down the length of the strands to smooth stray ends.

2. Place both strands in one hand, and extend your index finger between the two strands with your palm facing upward.

3. Turn your hand over so that your palm faces downward. This will twist the strands, and one strand will be positioned on top.

4. Now twist the top strand toward the center. Hold the strand firmly to maintain the twisted pattern and extend your index finger between the strands.

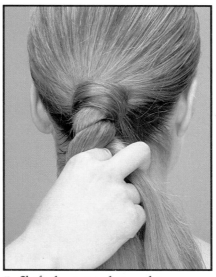

5. Shift the twisted strand to your right hand and turn your hand over, palm down, once again.

6. Twist the top strand, once again remembering to twist toward the center. Extend your index finger between the two strands.

(continued)

7. Shift the twisted strand so that your right hand holds both strands, and then turn your hand over so that your palm faces downward.

8. Repeat this pattern down the length of the strand. Maintain tension on the hair to keep the twist from unraveling.

9. Finish the ends by securing them with a covered band or spiral-wrapping them with a cord as shown here (see page 7).

Once you have created a two-strand rope with the ends of a ponytail, it can be coiled into a chignon or bun. As in all chignon designs, the main requirement is hair that is long enough to encircle the base of the ponytail. This design features a chignon in the nape, but the chignon can also be positioned in the crown or in the top of the head.

Position a ponytail in the location you would like for the chignon and create a two-strand rope with the free ends. Wrap the rope around the base of the ponytail to form a chignon. Tuck the ends underneath. Insert hairpins at the edge of the chignon to hold it in position as you adjust the final shape.

ELEGANT STATURE
TWISTED ROLL

This design is perfect for hair that has some degree of natural texture. You can also add curl to straight hair to give the texture necessary to make this design work well. The twisted rolls along the hairline join together at the nape in a free-falling braid. With shorter hair, the twisted roll can be positioned around the hairline and connect at the center back for one continuous roll. Add a hairpiece at the nape to form into a twist, roll, or chignon. Be creative!

1. Part the hair. Here, a side part was chosen. Define a large triangular section.

2. Direct this section back and away from the hairline. Lightly twist. Don't overtwist; overtwisting will give you a tighter shape with less volume.

3. With your index finger, pick up a new section from the hairline area. Direct it upward and into your hand. If the hair is long, comb through it with your hand to keep clean, controlled sections.

4. Lightly twist these newly joined sections.

5. Continue picking up hair from along the hairline.

6. Lift it upward and direct it into your other hand.

7. Twist lightly.

8. Curve around the hairline area as shown. Note the clear distribution of the hair at the top.

9. Pin the roll with a large bobby pin at the center back before moving to the opposite side to continue with the same procedure.

10. On the opposite side, section a triangular area of bangs. If you prefer loose bangs, pick up your first new section behind the bangs.

11. Direct this section back along the hairline, letting the hair's natural wave patterns bounce in, if you wish.

12. Continue the twist-and-roll technique. Pick up hair at the hairline.

(continued)

13. Add this new section to the opposite hand.

14. Turn the hand to create a twisted roll pattern.

15. Upon reaching the center back, pin the twisted roll in place securely.

16. These loose ends can be finished off in many ways. We've chosen to underbraid to the ends. Reach under to the outside left strand and cross this strand under the center strand.

17. Reach under with the thumb and index finger to the right strand and cross it under the center to the middle position. Alternate from side to side, using this underbraiding technique.

18. When you reach the very end, fasten with a covered band. Add ornamentation to this design to fit the occasion.